ANIMAL BATTLES

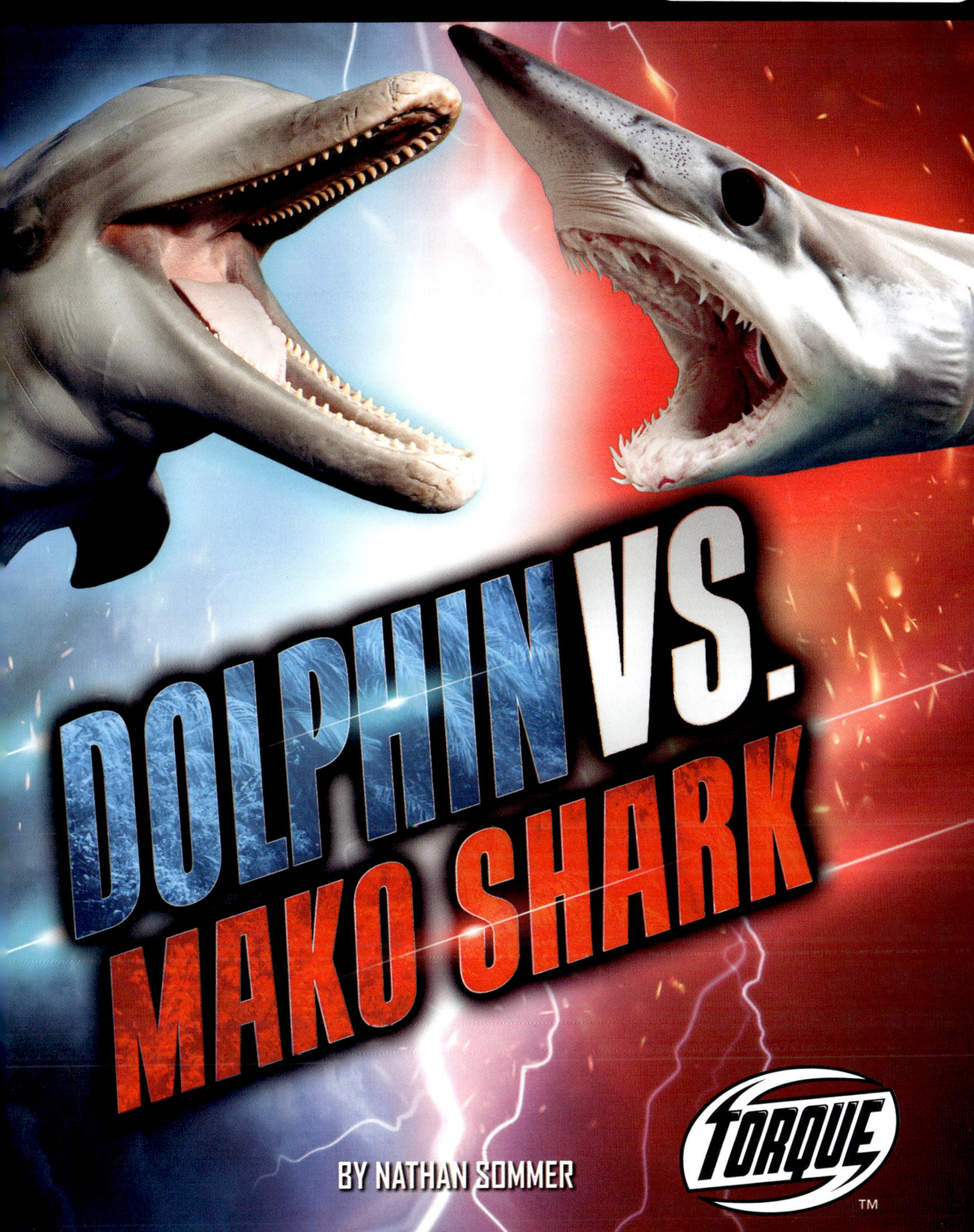

DOLPHIN VS. MAKO SHARK

TORQUE™

BY NATHAN SOMMER

TORQUE, AN IMPRINT OF BELLWETHER MEDIA BY FLUTTERBEE

Torque brims with excitement perfect for thrill-seekers of all kinds. Discover daring survival skills, explore uncharted worlds, and marvel at mighty engines and extreme sports. In *Torque* books, anything can happen. Are you ready?

This edition first published in 2026 by Bellwether Media, Inc.

For information regarding permission, write to Bellwether Media, Inc., Attention: Permissions Department, 3500 American Blvd W, Suite 150, Bloomington, MN 55431.

Library of Congress Cataloging-in-Publication Data is available at www.loc.gov or upon request from the publisher.

ISBN: 9798893048346 (hardcover)
ISBN: 9798898800147 (paperback)
ISBN: 9798893049343 (ebook)

Editor: Suzane Nguyen Designer: Josh Brink Series Designer: Andrea Schneider

Printed in the United States of America, North Mankato, MN.

TABLE OF CONTENTS

THE COMPETITORS

Many animals are found in the world's oceans. Dolphins are some of the smartest among them. These **mammals** use their **intelligence** to hunt **prey**.

Dolphins share the waters with mako sharks. These **apex predators** use their speed and powerful bite to easily defeat most prey. But which animal really rules the seas?

COMMON BOTTLENOSE DOLPHIN PROFILE

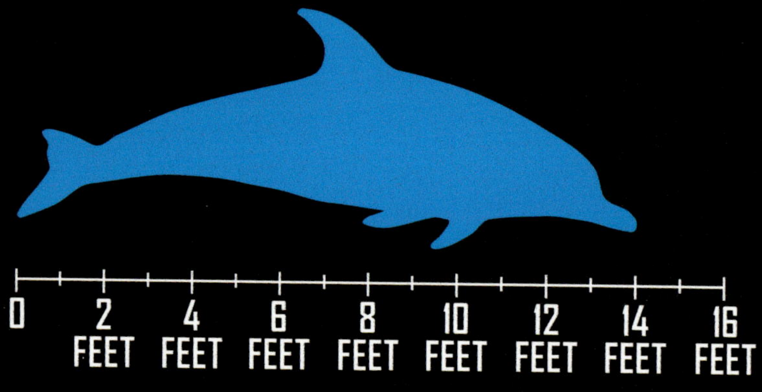

LENGTH

UP TO 14 FEET
(4.3 METERS)

WEIGHT

UP TO 1,400 POUNDS
(635 KILOGRAMS)

HABITATS

WARM OCEANS

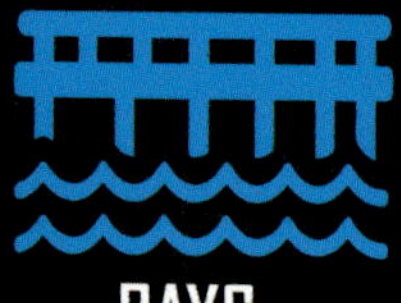

BAYS

HARBORS

COMMON BOTTLENOSE DOLPHIN RANGE

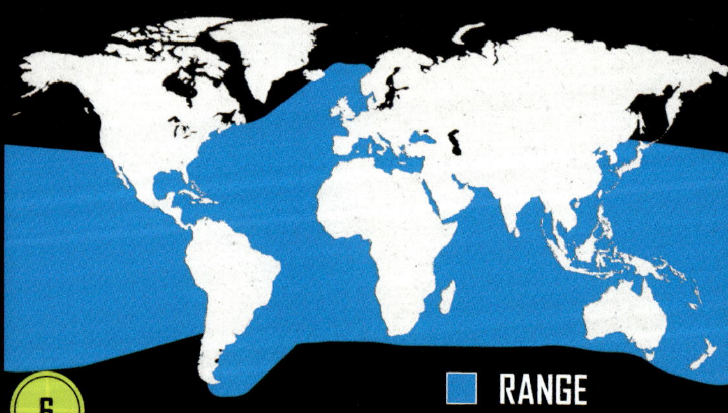

Dolphins are types of whales. They have long, sleek bodies. They have two **flippers** and powerful tail fins. Their short, thick **snouts** have curved mouths.

Dolphins are found in nearly every ocean. Many prefer warm waters near coastlines. They live in **pods** that can have thousands of members.

Mako sharks are large and speedy. They have slender, grayish-blue bodies. They have large eyes and pointed snouts. Their long, narrow teeth often stick out of their closed mouths.

Mako sharks live and hunt alone. The sharks are found in the warm, open waters of oceans. They usually swim between the surface and 490 feet (149 meters) below.

TRAVELING SHARKS

Mako sharks swim long distances. Some travel nearly 12,000 miles (19,312 kilometers) per year!

SHORTFIN MAKO SHARK PROFILE

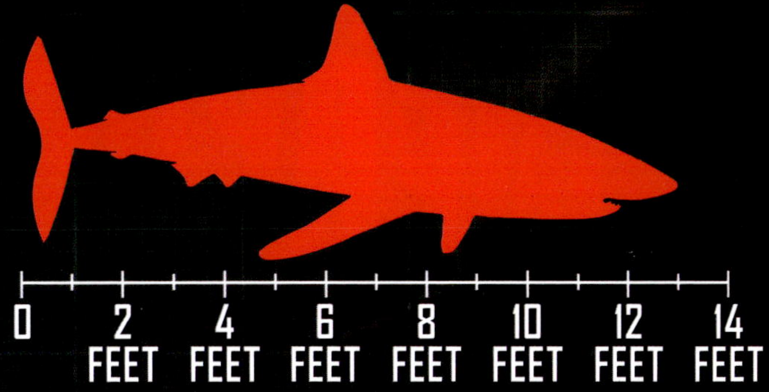

LENGTH

UP TO 13 FEET (4 METERS)

WEIGHT

UP TO 1,200 POUNDS (544 KILOGRAMS)

HABITATS

WARM OCEANS

OPEN SEAS

SHORTFIN MAKO SHARK PROFILE

SECRET WEAPONS

DIGGING DOLPHINS

Some dolphins carry sponges in their mouths. They use them to dig for prey under the sand.

Dolphins are intelligent. They are quick learners with great problem-solving skills. Some even use tools to hunt! They can easily find and outsmart their prey.

TOP SPEED

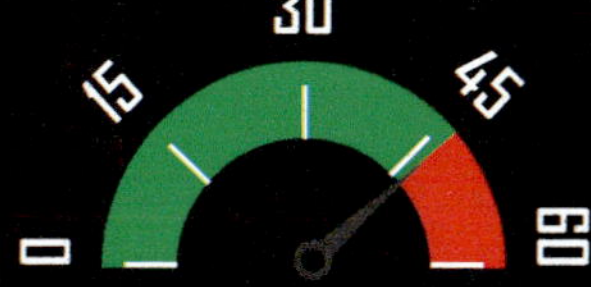

46 MILES (74 KILOMETERS) PER HOUR

MAKO SHARK

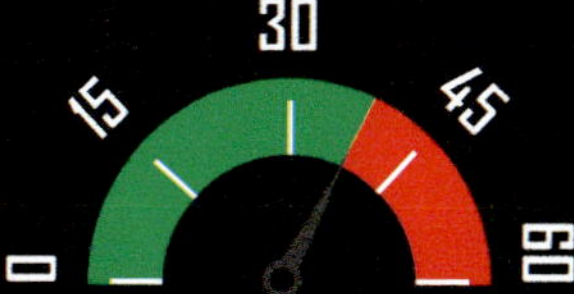

40 MILES (64.4 KILOMETERS) PER HOUR

FISHING BOAT

Mako sharks are the world's fastest sharks. They reach speeds of up to 46 miles (74 kilometers) per hour. Most prey cannot outswim them!

SECRET WEAPONS

DOLPHIN

Dolphins use **echolocation** to hunt. They make clicking sounds to talk to their pod members. This helps them plan their hunts and stay together.

Mako sharks can **thermoregulate**. This keeps their bodies warmer than the water. It allows them to see better and be more **agile** than other fish.

LEAPING DISTANCE

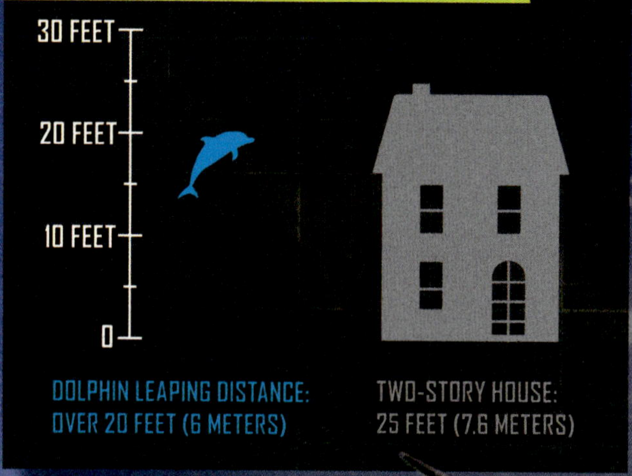

30 FEET
20 FEET
10 FEET
0

DOLPHIN LEAPING DISTANCE:
OVER 20 FEET (6 METERS)

TWO-STORY HOUSE:
25 FEET (7.6 METERS)

Streamlined bodies make dolphins agile swimmers. The fastest dolphins can reach speeds of up to 37 miles (60 kilometers) per hour. They can leap over 20 feet (6 meters) out of the water!

Mako sharks have large mouths with strong jaws. Inside are multiple rows of sharp teeth that curve backward. The sharks pack one of the world's strongest bites.

ATTACK MOVES

Dolphins use echolocation to find food. They make sounds that bounce off nearby objects and prey. Their lower jaws take in the returning sound waves. They know exactly where prey is!

Mako sharks use their speed to **ambush** prey. They often attack prey from below. The sharks bite off tails and fins first. This stops fish from escaping.

SHARK EATERS

Mako sharks eat whatever they can catch. They even eat other types of sharks!

EXCELLENT MEMORIES

Dolphins have long memories. They can recognize other dolphins they have not seen in over 20 years.

Dolphin pods hunt together. Some dolphins swim in a circle and use their tails to kick up mud. This traps their prey. They swallow fish that try to escape.

Sometimes mako sharks leap from the water when hunting. They ram their bodies quickly into prey. Then the sharks bite and tear apart their meals!

A dolphin digs for prey. A mako shark spots the dolphin. The dolphin sees the shark. It whistles to call its pod. The pod fights the shark.

The dolphins try to swim away. But the shark traps one of the dolphins in its strong jaws. The shark has won today!

GLOSSARY

agile—able to move quickly and easily

ambush—to carry out a surprise attack

apex predators—animals at the top of the food chain that are not preyed upon by other animals

echolocation—a way of locating objects using reflected sound waves

flippers—wide, flat body parts that are used for swimming

intelligence—the ability to learn or understand

mammals—warm-blooded animals that have backbones and feed their young milk

pods—groups of dolphins

prey—animals that are hunted by other animals for food

snouts—the nose and mouth areas on some animals

streamlined—shaped to move through water easily

thermoregulate—to control body temperature using a special group of blood vessels

TO LEARN MORE

AT THE LIBRARY

Adamson, Thomas K. *Great White Shark vs. Killer Whale.* Minneapolis, Minn.: Bellwether Media, 2020.

Boothroyd, Jennifer. *Mako Shark.* Minneapolis, Minn.: Bearport Publishing Company, 2022.

Eason, Sarah. *Pod Protection!: Supersmart Dolphins.* Minneapolis, Minn.: Bearport Publishing Company, 2023.

ON THE WEB

Factsurfer.com gives you a safe, fun way to find more information.

1. Go to www.factsurfer.com
2. Enter "dolphin vs. mako shark" into the search box and click 🔍.
3. Select your book cover to see a list of related content.

INDEX

The images in this book are reproduced through the courtesy of: Stephen Frink/ Getty Images, front cover (dolphin); Jessica Heim, front cover (mako shark); Nicolas-SB, pp. 2 (top right dolphins), 12 (intelligence), 21 (top right dolphins), 23 (top right dolphins); Andrea Izzotti, pp. 2 (left dolphin), 12 (echolocation), 20 (left dolphin), 22 (left dolphin); Brian Skerry/ Minden, pp. 3 (shark), 21 (shark), 23-24 (shark); coho, pp. 3 (bottom dolphin), 21 (bottom dolphin), 23-24 (bottom dolphin); Yeshaya, p. 4; wildestanimal, pp. 5, 18; jan stopka, pp. 6 (dolphin vector), 14 (dolphin vector); Tropicalens, pp. 6-7; Gail, pp. 8-9; AA.Stock, p. 9 (shark vector); HUBERT YANN/ Alamy Stock Photo, p. 10; Alessandro De Maddalena, p. 11; Tory Kallman, pp. 12 (streamlined body), 14; grafxart, p. 12; Richard Robinson/ Alamy Stock Photo, p. 13 (speed); Mark Chivers/ Getty Images, p. 13 (thermoregulation); MARK CONLIN/ VWPICS/ Alamy Stock Photo, p. 13 (powerful bite); David Salvatori/ AP Newsroom, p. 13; Andy Murch/ VWPics/ Newscom, p. 15; Jeff Rotman/ Alamy Stock Photo, p. 16; Richard Herrmann/ Minden, p. 17; Mark Metcalfe/ Getty Images, p. 19.